A DAY IN AN ECOSYSTEM

24 HOURS IN A LAKE

ALICIA Z. KLEPEIS

Cavendish Square
New York

Published in 2018 by Cavendish Square Publishing, LLC
243 5th Avenue, Suite 136, New York, NY 10016

Library of Congress Cataloging-in-Publication Data

Names: Klepeis, Alicia, 1971- author.
Title: 24 hours in a lake / Alicia Z. Klepeis.
Other titles: Twenty-four hours in a lake
Description: New York : Cavendish Square Publishing, 2018. | Series: A day in an ecosystem | Includes index.
Identifiers: LCCN 2016050107 (print) | LCCN 2016055748 (ebook) | ISBN 9781502624802 (library bound) | ISBN 9781502624819 (E-book)
Subjects: LCSH: Lake ecology--Juvenile literature.
Classification: LCC QH541.5.L3 K54 2018 (print) | LCC QH541.5.L3 (ebook) | DDC 577.63--dc23
LC record available at https://lccn.loc.gov/2016050107

Editorial Director: David McNamara
Editor: Fletcher Doyle
Copy Editor: Rebecca Rohan
Associate Art Director: Amy Greenan
Designer: Stephanie Flecha
Production Coordinator: Karol Szymczuk
Photo Research: J8 Media

Printed in the United States of America

CONTENTS

DAWN

IT'S early morning. As you wander down to the lakeshore from your campsite, your feet crunch on pine needles. Squirrels scamper about, looking for their next meal. You arrive at the water's edge. The sky is streaked with yellow and orange. But the lake itself looks like a mirror, almost silvery. You see and hear ripples as the water laps the shore. Where are you? On the shore of Lake Superior. Lake Superior is one of the Great Lakes. It is also one of the largest lakes in the world.

There are millions of lakes around the globe. Lakes are bodies of water surrounded by land. Most lakes contain freshwater, though there are salt water lakes as well. The salt in the lake water may come from nearby minerals, such as in the Great Salt Lake. Lakes vary greatly in size. Some are so small they can fit in someone's backyard. Small lakes are often called ponds but there is no size limit on what can be called a pond. The Caspian **Sea**, located in Asia and Europe, is the world's largest lake by

 Waves lap the rocky shore at sunrise on Lake Superior, which is the largest of the five Great Lakes and one of the largest lakes in the world.

area (143,244 square miles or 371,000 square kilometers). It has salty water. Sometimes salty lakes, or big lakes, have wrongly been called seas. **Meres** are big, shallow lakes commonly found in the United Kingdom. Each of these bodies of water has its own unique features yet they are all lakes.

Different plants and animals live in and around lakes from Peru to Russia. Birds stop at lakes on their annual migration routes. River otters or beavers may make their homes here. Frogs and salamanders might creep about the muddy shoreline. Fish of all shapes and sizes swim in search of food and mates. Some plants peek out above the lake's surface. Others may be held by their roots to the lake bottom. Tens of thousands of species of plants and animals live in the world's lakes. Some are not found anywhere else.

In this book, you will get a chance to explore Lake Superior. It's the biggest of all the Great Lakes, bordering the northern edge of Wisconsin, the eastern edge of Minnesota, the upper peninsula of Michigan, and the Canadian province of Ontario.

Lake Superior and its surrounding lands are home to all kinds of birds, fish, other animals and plants. Each creature or plant depends on the others for survival. An ecosystem includes all of the living things in a particular area, which interact with one another, as well as with their environment (including the nonliving parts like soil, water, sunlight, and so on).

This watercolor-style map shows the state of Michigan, including its Upper Peninsula, which borders three of the Great Lakes.

A pine marten peers out from its perch These furry animals often nest in trees.

AMERICAN MARTEN

If you're out and about at dawn, you might see an American marten near the shore. This mammal is related to otters, weasels, and minks (among others). American martens are solitary unless it's mating season. An adult male is 20 to 25 inches (50 to 64 cm) long, and weighs less than 3 pounds (1.36 kilograms). They often prey on red squirrels, but they will eat birds, fish, frogs, insects, fruit, and nuts, too.

Lake Superior is about 160 miles (257 kilometers) from north to south and 350 miles (563 km) from west to east. Within the lake are a number of islands, including the Apostle Islands and Isle Royale. Both belong to the US National Park Service. Around the lake are forests, cliffs, and shorelines, all of which provide homes to many incredible animals and plants.

Did you hear that "kraak" sound a minute ago? That was the call of the great blue heron. Someone in the campground probably startled it in mid-flight. If you want to see birds or other wildlife, it's a good idea not to talk too loudly. Hold on—it looks like the heron is coming down to the lake for a landing. Great blue herons are most active at dawn and dusk. The heron scoops up water with its yellowish bill, then tips it head back to drink. After it takes a drink, the heron looks to be stabbing something with its spearlike bill. From this distance, it's hard to see what the heron is eating. It might be a frog, a crayfish, or perhaps a larger fish. After feeding, the heron flaps its mighty gray wings and heads up, up, up. It may be returning to its stick nest high in a nearby tree.

Even though it's early July, you may want a light jacket or sweatshirt in the morning. Temperatures are likely to be in the 50s before the sun gets high in the sky. By the afternoon, the weather is likely to be around 70 degrees Fahrenheit (21 degrees Celsius), perfect for exploring. Be sure to bring a life jacket, some knee-high rubber boots, and a camera for your trip around Lake Superior.

What's next? You never know what you'll see from moment to moment.

MORNING

GRAB your backpack. It's time to have a little bite to eat. As you make your way to what looks like a tree stump, you nearly tread on an eastern garter snake. Eew! What's that smell? The snake must have been frightened enough that it let off a stinky, musky odor from glands near its tail. This snake was about 1.5 feet long (46 centimeters), though they can grow as long as 3 feet (92 cm) or more.

It's not common to run into snakes around Lake Superior. They tend to keep themselves hidden from view. One of the park rangers who will be taking you around today says that there aren't many reptiles and amphibians here at Pictured Rocks National Lakeshore, on the south shore of the lake. This park is pretty far north. Cold-blooded animals tend to live in warmer climates.

You get to the stump and are surrounded by a variety of trees. This spot seems to have lots of maple and beech trees. Along the lakeshore

Amazing rock formations are part of the scenery at Michigan's Pictured Rocks National Lakeshore.

This close-up shows the deeply colored fruit and tiny leaves of the Black Crowberry plant. Birds, voles, and black bears eat these berries.

are also upland forests where yellow birch and hemlock trees grow. Spruce, alder, and tamarack trees rise from the region's wetland soils.

Hiding in these trees are black bears. You wouldn't have seen them if your guide hadn't pointed them out with her binoculars. Visitors are not likely to run into any, though they sometimes find bear **scat** while exploring. A large variety of **mammals** live in and around Lake Superior.

Before you get too far into your adventures, you mention that you are doing a school project on the flowers and aquatic plants of the Lake Superior area. One of your guides is a botanist, a scientist who studies plants. You follow her as she hikes to a sheltered, cool pocket of forest. She squats down and points out a creeping, low evergreen shrub. It has barely visible purple flowers. This plant, known as the black crowberry or arctic crowberry, won't bear fruit until later in the summer. But what's amazing is that this plant can survive way up north in Canada.

A pair of painted turtles basks in the morning sunshine on a log.

Bears sometimes enjoy these berries. You wish you could have tried them. Maybe next summer.

Back at the shore, the sun is starting to warm you a bit. But look, the sun is also warming something else: a few painted turtles are lying on a fallen log. They are basking, or exposing themselves to light and warmth. If they get too hot, they'll move along. Painted turtles are quite colorful, as their name implies. Their lower shell (known as the plastron) has red and yellow patterns on it. They have orange, red, and yellow stripes on their legs and neck.

Snapping turtles can also be seen in the area. From May through July, these turtles dig nests in the well-drained, sandy soils here. They have been known to deposit one hundred eggs in a nest, though twenty to forty is the average. They don't venture into Lake Superior often, though. You can't really blame them. After all, the average temperature (for the year) in the lake is 40°F (4.4°C). Brrr! This is colder than any of the other Great Lakes, which are further south.

You might wonder how people can swim in Lake Superior if it's so cold. One thing that's important to keep in mind is how deep this lake is. At its

Ice covers Lake Superior at Wisconsin's Apostle Islands. Ice caves sometimes form in the winter here.

DOES LAKE SUPERIOR FREEZE?

Even though Lake Superior is big and deep, parts of it freeze over every winter. During most winters, between 40 and 95 percent of the lake is covered with ice. But it's unusual for the entire lake to freeze over. In February of 2015, Lake Superior was 95.5 percent covered in ice. Brrr!

deepest point, Lake Superior is 1,300 feet (400 meters) below its surface. In the summertime, the sun warms the surface waters of the lake to almost 70°F (21°C). The bottom of the lake stays cold. A swimmer might be able to notice the sharp difference in temperature, known as the **thermocline**. The warm surface layer of water is called the **epilimnion**. The deep, cold (bottom) layer of water is the **hypolimnion**.

Water temperature affects fish all day, every day. It controls the body temperature of the fish. It also controls when and how much they eat. Fish are cold-blooded animals. So if the lake water is cold, the fishes' body temperature will be cold. Fish like bass will be sluggish if the lake water is too cold. Under these conditions, they will need less food because their bodies will be slower at digesting it.

Each fish species has its own preferred water temperatures. At these preferred temperatures, the fish are active and can grow, reproduce, and digest food efficiently. For example, lake trout

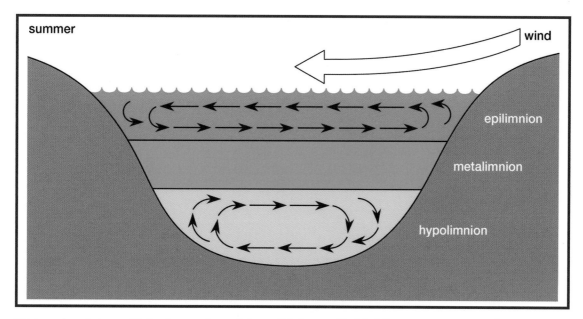

Water circulates within layers in a lake, which are divided by temperature. The metalimnion, between the colder and warmer layers, changes temperature rapidly.

are most comfortable between 48°F and 52°F (8.9°C to 11.1°C).

If the surface water is too warm, fish that prefer cooler temperatures will go deeper. Likewise, if the lower lake water is too cool, fish will migrate upward to warmer waters.

While some fish become more active during the daytime, they often feed at dawn or dusk. The cooler water temperatures of the early morning and the late afternoon allow fish to swim in shallow water to find food. These are usually the best times for you to go fishing. However, you have other plans for today.

A double-crested cormorant spreads its wings to dry them in the sunlight. It is standing on a pipe.

You put on your lifejacket. Your guides have borrowed canoes to explore some of the nearby shoreline. Birdcalls come from all around. At first you cannot see any birds in flight or on the water. And then, all of a sudden, a large brownish-black waterbird comes from out of nowhere. Your guide whispers that it's a double-crested cormorant. Perhaps it has flown in from its nest on a nearby island. Double-crested cormorants make stick nests high up in trees.

The bird skims the water's surface before diving in. When the cormorant emerges from the lake, you expect it to have a large fish in its thin, hooked beak. But it has caught something else—a crayfish. The cormorant doesn't just gulp down its meal. First it hammers the crayfish against the water, then flips it into the air before catching it headfirst and swallowing it. After its feeding show, the cormorant flies to a rock. It spreads its wings wide. It does this to dry its feathers after diving for prey.

Your guides paddle on a little farther. In the distance you see some yellow pond lilies. Some insects and frogs attach their egg masses to the leaves and stems of this plant during breeding season (in spring). Other animals, like beavers, eat the leaves and the **rhizomes** of these lilies. Fish, insects, and other water creatures use the lilies as cover or a landing spot. Speaking of landing, you're almost at your next stop.

A wood frog sits on moss in its habitat. These frogs usually don't live more than three years in the wild.

WOOD FROG

You might be surprised to see a "burglar" near Lake Superior. Wood frogs have a black marking over their eyes that looks like a burglar's mask. They lay their eggs in the water. Wood frogs produce a natural "antifreeze" that keeps their cells from dying when the water in their bodies freezes during the cold winters.

AFTERNOON

YOU help your guides paddle a little farther along the coast. The water is pretty calm. The sun is high in the sky now. You arrive at an area that has loads of plants growing. It's a marsh. Marshes are areas of low, wet land often found at the edges of lakes and streams. Some of the plants seem to be floating on the water's surface. You can see from the canoe that there are also lots of plants growing beneath the top of the lake. Aquatic plants provide habitats for many **invertebrates**, which in turn are eaten by fish, amphibians, ducks, and so on.

Coontail is a dark, olive-green colored plant that does not have roots in the bottom of the lakebed. It grows in dense colonies. Why is it called coontail? The tips of this plant's branches are crowded with leaves so it resembles the tail of a raccoon, a resident mammal that comes out at night.

This close-up of coontail shows its bushy leaf structure. This plant grows all over the US and Canada.

The fluffy seed heads of these cattails will blow across the lake in autumn. Cattails prefer to grow in shallow, flooded conditions.

Once the canoe has pulled up to the shore, you slip on your tall rubber boots so that you can wade a bit through the marsh. Because the water is very clear, you crouch down a bit to see what lies below the surface. Eelgrass is growing here. The blades of this grass are up to three feet long. Tiny fish swim in and out among its blades. Eelgrass is a type of plant known as a **submergent** plant, meaning that all parts of it are underwater. Another submergent plant is pondweed. Plants like this help to hold the surface sands of the lake in place. They also provide both shelter and food for a variety of wildlife.

A number of **emergent** plants also grow near the shoreline in this marsh. Emergent plants have roots in the lake bottom, but their stems and leaves extend beyond the water's surface. You have seen cattails in a pond near your house. Their leaves are flat and long, but their flower is shaped like a cigar. Right now, the flower is green but it will turn brown and fuzzy in the fall. Muskrats and beavers eat their roots and stalks. Marsh birds sometimes use patches of cattails both for cover and as a nesting site.

A fierce northern pike has caught a small fish and holds its prey in its very sharp teeth.

Behind the cattail fringe, the northern pike sometimes **spawn**. Many fishermen hope to catch these fish, as they are prized for their tasty white flesh. The northern pike is a **predator** fish. It may stay motionless for hours while waiting for **prey**. But as soon as a small fish gets close —bam—the pike strikes. The northern pike is known for its needle-like teeth. Northern pike seem to be hungry all the time. They lunge at nearly any lure that comes their way. But look out! This fish can be as much as 60 inches (1.5 m) long. That's about the height of a typical twelve-year-old girl!

After hearing about the northern pike, you are glad you didn't see one while wading in the shallows. You'd prefer to see a big fish from inside a fishing boat. Speaking of fishing, you notice a boat carrying a family just beyond the area with the cattails and yellow pond lilies. They seem to be swatting at themselves. Come to think of it, you have also gotten a few mosquito bites today. It's a good thing you put on some bug repellent before you headed out this morning. Otherwise you might be covered in bites.

The green-striped darner, a large dragonfly, is often found in marshy areas.

One of your guides commends you for using repellent and wearing long pants and a long-sleeve top. These will help to ward off the curse of Lake Superior: the deerflies and horseflies that arrive in midsummer. The females of these varieties fly in fast and noisy circles around their victims before inflicting a painful bite. Ouch! When you spy a few dragonflies darting about, you breathe a sigh of relief. Why? They eat mosquitoes. Also, they're really fun to watch since they come in many different colors. You decide your favorite is the Green Darner. Dragonflies are quite acrobatic when they move about and can fly backward and forward. They are most active during the heat of the day.

You get back in the canoe and paddle a little farther along the shoreline toward a dock. Your guides tell you a little more about Lake Superior's **littoral zone**. This is the area near the shore where sunlight can penetrate down to the sediment at the bottom of the lake. Aquatic plants can grow here. You also see **algae**. These living organisms vary in size. Algae are very important to any ecosystem. Using sunlight, they produce their own food by a process called **photosynthesis**. This process releases oxygen into the air. Lots of water animals eat algae. Also, oxygen is essential for animals to breathe. Many invertebrates and fish live and feed in the littoral zone. It's full of life.

Just before you arrive at the shore, one of your guides points out a plant with tiny pink

A killdeer searches for food in shallow water. These birds mainly eat invertebrates like worms and insects.

A PIERCING CRY

Killdeer are among the many shorebirds that live along the Lake Superior waterfront. These medium-sized birds have two dark bands on their upper breast. They get their name from their piercing loud cry that sounds like "kill-dee(r)." They can live in savannas and forests, but they prefer open areas. You are likely to find one on a sandbar.

The pink flowers of the flowering rush are in blossom by the water's edge. This plant is between 1 foot and 4 feet (30.5 to 122 centimeters) tall.

flowers. This plant, known as flowering rush, grows to about 3 feet tall (.9 m). In shallow parts of lakes, it grows as an emergent. But it can also grow as a submergent plant in water that's up to 10 feet (3 m) deep. Flowering rush is an **invasive** species that came from Europe and Asia. It grows in dense stands and tends to crowd native species out of the way.

Once on land, you quickly store your canoe. There's a nearby dock with a line of people. They are waiting to go to Isle Royale, the largest island in Lake Superior. You've never been on a seaplane before. One of your guides will accompany you to the island, but the other will stay behind.

You board the small seaplane, not sure what to expect. Once up in the air, you get a real sense of how huge Lake Superior is. From above, it sometimes looks like the ocean. The flight is short, but the views are sensational!

LONG-LASTING POLLUTION

Lakes around the world have problems with pollution. Mercury and dioxin, both found in Lake Superior, can harm wildlife. Even though Lake Superior has the cleanest water of all the Great Lakes, it faces a challenge. Water that enters Lake Superior takes about 191 years to make its way out, so any cleanup requires a long effort.

EVENING

YOUR seaplane makes a smooth landing at a dock. You are lucky—sometimes the waters of Lake Superior can be rough. The calmest months of the year are June and July, while the stormiest tend to be October and November. And while Lake Superior does not have tides like the oceans, it does have waves. Winds can cause huge waves on this lake, especially in the fall.

Isle Royale is not the only island within Lake Superior. In fact, Isle Royale National Park is an archipelago (a group of islands) of about four hundred islands. Isle Royale is a nature lover's paradise. Your guide tells you that this national park is one of the least visited in the country. Part of this may be because you have to take a boat or a plane to get here. There are no roads on this 45-mile-long (72.5 km) island.

Since it's summer, you still have some light left to explore. You meet the park ranger who will be taking you to see some of the island's plants and

The rocky, forested coastline of Isle Royale National Park, located in Lake Superior, is dangerous to boaters.

A white-tailed deer comes down to the lakeshore to take a drink of water.

animals. With 165 miles of trails, there's a lot to see! The rocky, tree-lined coastline features many **conifers**, trees that have cones and scalelike or needlelike leaves.

Just minutes into your hike, you see deer scat. At this time of year, white-tailed deer have reddish-brown fur with white patches on their lower legs and faces. (In the winter, their fur can be more grayish.) They are often munching grass, the new leaves of shrubs and trees, and flowering plants like bunchberry.

White-tailed deer are good swimmers. It's not unusual for them to enter lakes to escape insects or predators or to visit islands. Since Isle Royale contains forty-six lakes, you *could* find a deer swimming. But usually deer

Large, lichen-dotted rocks jut out into Lake Superior at Isle Royale National Park, which is close to the Canadian border.

are shy—you might catch the white underside of their tails as they bound away from people.

The idea of swimming after a hike sounds appealing. But then you recall that you read there are leeches in some of the lakes on Isle Royale. The weedy, rocky shorelines of these lakes can also be hard to navigate. Much like lakes all over the region, people here fish, kayak, and canoe for recreation. You may notice a couple of artists painting and sketching the scenery as well.

You continue up the trail. For a time, the woods seem to enclose you. The leaves of a paper birch flutter in the light breeze. White-throated sparrows sing from the branches of a nearby bush. They call repeatedly to one another with their high-pitched melodies. Your guide quietly points out the sparrow's bright yellow patch between its eyes and its bill.

The forest you are walking through is called a **boreal** forest. These are northern forests of mostly conifers. Balsam fir, mountain ash, and white spruce are some of the trees growing along the island's rugged shoreline. Lake Superior creates cool and moist weather conditions in the areas right around it. These encourage the growth of boreal forests. Further inland are drier and warmer conditions where forests of Northern hardwoods grow. Yellow birches and sugar maples grow in these hardwood forests.

Now and again, you stop in your tracks and get out your camera to take pictures for your school project. One of your favorites is the twinflower, with

This beautiful **purple fairy slipper** orchid is just one of many orchids found in the Lake Superior area.

its pink to white bell-shaped flowers. You take a deep sniff—these flowers smell great! Another great flower is the harebell, often called a "bluebell" for its vibrant color. The botanist guide traveling with you says her favorite flower to see on Isle Royale is the calypso orchid. But they bloom in the early spring, so it's too late for this year to spy their lavender and white flowers.

Just as you put your camera back in your bag, the park ranger puts his index finger to his lips. At first, you aren't sure why. You see him point ahead and to the left. It's hard to see with all the trees. You squint your eyes, trying to focus. And then, about 100 yards (30 m) in the distance, you see a moose! Its giant hooves seem to thunder on the ground as it clomps around in search of food. Moose, like deer, are most active at dawn or dusk. This means they are **crepuscular**.

This enormous animal is the largest member of the deer family. Moose can weigh up to 1,800 pounds (828 kg) and can stand much taller than an adult man. Moose are **herbivores** and eat all kinds of plants, from ripe

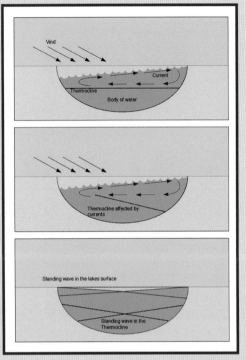

This illustration shows what happens to the lake water level during a seiche.

TILTING THE WATER

The water in lakes, bays, and gulfs does not stay still. A seiche is temporary oscillation in the water level of a lake. Winds push the water level of the lake up at one end and drop the water level by the same amount at the other end.

red thimbleberries to water lilies to pine cones and tree buds. During summertime, moose are often seen eating aquatic plants, both above and below the water's surface. You look through your guide's binoculars. It looks like this moose is using its hooves to clear patches in search of mosses and lichens.

After a few minutes, the moose moves on, deeper into the forest. Soon the coast is clear. Moose are very strong, capable of killing someone with a powerful kick. These giant creatures are also good swimmers and have been known to paddle for several miles in one journey. Your guide shows you something known as "moose browse." This is a place where shrubs and trees have been stunted by years of moose feeding there.

Before the light gets too dim, there's a spot your guide wants to show you. It's a beaver pond. Beavers are often residents of lakes and ponds around the world. These hard-working mammals change a landscape more than many

Two moose swim in a lake. Moose came to Isle Royale by swimming to it in the early 1900s.

other animals do. They use their sharp teeth to gnaw and fell trees, blocking streams and turning forests or even fields into ponds for their own use. Besides trees, leaves, and bark, they also eat aquatic plants.

You spy a beaver lodge (or home) in the middle of the pond. The beavers can get inside from an underwater entrance. These giant rodents can weigh 60 pounds (27 kg).

It's time to head back toward the lakefront for a last adventure or two.

STAY AWAY, SNAILS!

Snails live in many lakes. Some snails are native, while others are invasive species. The New Zealand mudsnail is just one invasive example found in Lake Superior. About the size of a peppercorn, these invaders can push out other native snails, insects, and other invertebrates that are important food sources for fish.

NIGHT

YOU arrive at a cabin right next to the lakeshore. A couple of park rangers are cooking some fish they caught after work. They are chatting amongst themselves. The fish might be a cisco or a lake trout or a yellow perch. From where you're standing, it's hard to tell.

Since you have a couple of minutes before dinner is ready, you take out your journal to add a few notes from this trip. You forgot to mention that last night you had a run-in with a raccoon family. It was dark out, and you were heading to brush your teeth and get ready for bed in the campground. You heard the rattling of a garbage can and thought your older brother was messing with you. He knows you don't like being in the woods after dark. You stood still and used your flashlight to see what you could spy. A couple of raccoons had gotten the lid off the barrel and were helping themselves to food scraps left from campers. In the distance, some other raccoons were drinking water from the lake.

A raccoon wanders about during the daylight. Usually raccoons are nocturnal

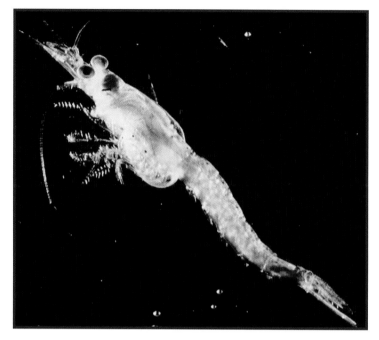

This is a close-up of an opossum shrimp. These animals are less than an inch (2.5 cm) long.

Raccoons are excellent swimmers and will hunt frogs, fish, and crayfish (among other creatures).

It's time for dinner. You put away your journal. The rangers take the fish off the grill. It's delicious.

Lakes around the world are home to a huge variety of fish. Lake Superior is home to about eighty-eight fish species, if you include the wetlands and **estuaries** around the lake. Some fish stay in the shallows and live close to the shoreline. Others are deepwater dwellers. Kiyi live in Lake Superior's depths. At night they rise from the shadowy lake bottom, following their prey, *Mysis* (the opossum shrimp). *Mysis* rise to the upper levels of the lake at night to feed on **plankton**.

Plankton are tiny living organisms that drift and float in oceans and other water bodies like lakes. There are two main kinds of plankton:

phytoplankton (made of plants or plantlike organisms) and **zooplankton** (made of animals or animal-like organisms). These tiny organisms are at the bottom or base of the food chain. Small fish and other creatures eat them, and then in turn are eaten by bigger fish, birds, or other animals.

Both *Mysis* and Kiyi sink back to the lake bottom in the morning. In the course of their rising and descending, these animals cross through all three major zones of a lake: the **littoral**, **limnetic** or photic, and **profundal** or aphotic zones. In the limnetic zone, there is enough light to penetrate the water so that plant and animal plankton can survive there. Various freshwater fish also live there. By contrast, light cannot penetrate the

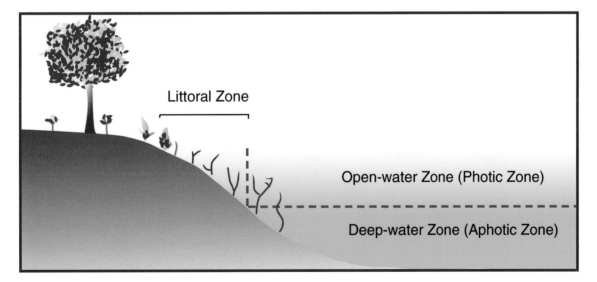

This diagram shows the three primary zones of a lake—littoral (near the shore), open-water (or photic), and deep-water (or aphotic).

water down to the lake's profundal zone. It is colder than the other two zones. Organisms that have adapted to the dark can thrive there.

Of all the Great Lakes, kiyi are only found in Lake Superior. But other fish are also more active at night. The walleye is one example. It prefers to dine in the early morning or late at night. Walleye eat pike, bass, trout, perch, and minnows (among others).

A lake sturgeon swims well below the water's surface. It uses its whisker-like barbels to locate bottom-dwelling prey.

When you ask the rangers what the biggest fish in Lake Superior is, they all smile, then take turns telling you about the lake sturgeon. Creatures of lore and legend, these fish are bottom-feeders. They are active at night. Lake sturgeon travel widely in search of food, dragging their **barbels** (whiskers) along the bottom to find prey. They eat many kinds of food, including insect larvae, snails, leeches, other invertebrates, and small fish. There are many remarkable things about lake sturgeon. Females can live more than 150 years. These fish have been around since the days of the dinosaurs, more than 150 million years. And lake sturgeon are huge: they can be 8 feet (2.4 m) long and weigh more than 300 pounds (136 kg)! You wish you could have seen one.

After your dinner and the chat about fish, your guides invite you to sit on their porch. They suggest you do something unusual: sit in the dark and just listen. At first, your eyes have trouble adjusting to the dark. But gradually

A red fox searches for food in the snow. It can hear prey like voles scampering under 3 feet (.9 m) of snow.

RED FOX

One of the most recognizable nocturnal animals around Lake Superior is the red fox. This skillful hunter can hear small animals that are digging under the ground and will dig through dirt or even snow to find their prey. In addition to eating mice and squirrels, red fox will also eat grasses, berries, beetles, crayfish, and more.

HOW MUCH WATER IS IN LAKE SUPERIOR?

You know Lake Superior is big. And deep. It contains more than half of all the water in the Great Lakes. Just how much water does it have? Lake Superior contains three quadrillion (3,000,000,000,000,000) gallons of water. That's enough water to submerge both North and South America under 1 foot (0.3 m) of water!

gradually you can make out the shapes of things better–starting with the bats that dart to and fro in front of the cabin and over the water at the shore. They may be having a mosquito and gnat feast. Who knows?

Just when you start to feel relaxed in the darkness, a spine-tingling sound startles you. Howwwwwl! Howwwwl! Could that be a wolf? Yes, it could. A number of wolves live on Isle Royale and in different parts of the Great Lakes basin. Wolves may seem scary, but they almost never attack humans. They are the biggest members of the dog family and can weigh up to 175 pounds (79 kg). Wolves are carnivores or meat-eaters. Here on Isle Royale, they might feed on white-tailed deer or snowshoe hares.

You're feeling pretty beat after a full day of exploring Lake Superior. You took lots of pictures, canoed, hiked, and rode in a seaplane. You'll get to spend one night in a cabin with your guides before you head

Clusters of bats take flight at nightfall, searching for their insect prey.

back to meet your family. You can't wait to explore more lakes on future trips. Maybe next time you'll get to see the Great Salt Lake in Utah or Crater Lake in Oregon. Every lake has its own plants, animals, and fascinating stories to tell.

WHERE ARE THE GREAT LAKES?

FAST FACTS ABOUT LAKES
(THE GREAT LAKES)

SIZE: Lakes come in many sizes, from a few square meters to more than 100,000 square miles (259,000 square kilometers). Lake Superior, the largest Great Lake, covers 31,699 square miles (82,100 sq km).

TEMPERATURE: In the Lake Superior region, the (high) temperatures average about 70°C (21°C) in the summer and about 22°F (–5.6°C) in the winter. The average temperature of the lake water itself is about 40°F (4°C).

PRECIPITATION (RAIN, SLEET, AND SNOW): The Lake Superior region averages about 30 inches (76 cm) of precipitation a year.

PLANTS FOUND IN AND AROUND LAKE SUPERIOR: *Trees* include birches, maples, mountain ash, pines, tamarack, white cedar, and white spruce. *Flowering plants* include harebells, thimbleberry, and nearly sixty species of orchids. *Aquatic plants* include coontail, flowering rush, and yellow pond lilies. There are also shrubs, ferns, rushes, lichens, and mosses.

ANIMALS FOUND IN AND AROUND LAKE SUPERIOR: *Amphibians* include green frogs, mink frogs, newts, salamanders, spring peepers, and wood frogs. *Birds* include bald eagles, double-crested cormorants, great blue herons, grebes, hawks, killdeer, loons, osprey, owls, and woodpeckers. Fish include brook trout, burbot, cisco, lake chub, lake sturgeon, northern pike, salmon, walleye, smallmouth bass, and yellow perch. Insects include beetles, black flies, butterflies, deerflies, dragonflies, gnats, mosquitoes, no-see-ums, and stable flies. Mammals include beavers, black bears, gray wolves, moose, North American raccoons, red squirrels, river otters, snowshoe hares, squirrels, weasels, and white-tailed deer. Reptiles include garter snakes, northern red-bellied snakes, and the western painted turtle. There are also many copepods, crayfish, mites, shrimp, snails, worms, and spiders.

POPULATION OF THE REGION: About 425,000 US citizens and 181,000 Canadians live in the Lake Superior basin.

GLOSSARY

algae A plant or plantlike organism (like seaweed) that includes forms mainly growing in water. They lack true stems, leaves, roots, and vascular tissue.

barbel A slender, fleshy filament (like a whisker) growing from the snout or mouth of a fish.

basin The land drained by a river and its branches or which drains into a lake or sea.

boreal Relating to the climatic zone south of the Arctic, particularly the cold temperate region dominated by forests of birch, poplar, and conifers.

carnivore An animal that eats flesh (meat).

conifer A tree that has cones and evergreen needlelike or scalelike leaves.

crepuscular An animal that is active at twilight.

emergent Of or denoting a water plant with flowers and leaves that appear above the water's surface.

epilimnion The upper layer of water in a lake that has layers of different temperatures.

estuary The tidal mouth of a large river, or the place where the tide meets a river current.

herbivore An animal that eats plants.

hypolimnion The lower layer of water in a stratified lake, which is usually cooler than the water above.

invasive A plant or animal that is not native to an ecosystem and that spreads widely and can be harmful.

invertebrate An animal lacking a backbone.

lichen A slow-growing, simple plant that usually forms a low crustlike or leaflike growth on walls, rocks, and trees.

limnetic The zone of a freshwater ecosystem above the profundal zone and inhabited mainly by plankton species.

littoral The zone close to shore where sunlight reaches the sediment, allowing plants to grow.

mammal A warm-blooded vertebrate that has fur or hair and nourishes its young with milk produced by the females. The offspring are born alive.

mere A lake, pond, or sheet of still water.

photosynthesis The process by which plants use sunlight to make food from carbon dioxide (in the air) and water.

phytoplankton Plankton made up of microscopic plants.

plankton The weakly swimming or floating animal and plant life of a water body.

predator An animal that lives by killing and eating other animals.

prey An animal that is hunted or killed by another animal for food.

profundal The deepest zone in a freshwater ecosystem where light does not effectively penetrate.

rhizome A rootlike and usually horizontal underground plant stem that produces roots below and shoots above.

scat The feces (poop) deposited by an animal.

sea An inland body of water, with either freshwater or salt water.

spawn To produce young, particularly in large numbers, or to deposit or fertilize eggs.

submergent A plant that lives completely underwater.

thermocline A steep temperature gradient in a lake, where the layer above and below are at different temperatures.

zooplankton Plankton made up of small animals and the immature stages of bigger animals.

FIND OUT MORE

Books

Fleisher, Paul. *Lake and Pond Food Webs in Action*. Minneapolis, MN: Lerner Classroom, 2013.

Johansson, Philip. *Lakes and Rivers: A Freshwater Web of Life*. New York: Enslow Elementary, 2007.

Kopp, Megan. *Rivers and Lakes Inside Out*. New York: Crabtree Publishing Company, 2015.

Miller, Mirella S. *Life in Freshwater Lakes*. North Mankato, MN: Child's World, 2014.

Websites

National Geographic Education: Lake

http://nationalgeographic.org/encyclopedia/lake

Learn what lakes are, how they are formed, and what animals and plants are commonly found on them, plus view many photos and fun facts about lakes.

National Wildlife Federation: Great Lakes

http://www.nwf.org/wildlife/wild-places/great-lakes.aspx

This website talks about the five Great Lakes, including how people use the lakes, what wildlife lives here, and what some threats to the lakes are. It also discusses invasive species.

Wisconsin Department of Natural Resources—Environmental Education for Kids: Lake Superior

http://dnr.wi.gov/org/caer/ce/eek/nature/habitat/lakesuperior.htm

This website gives loads of details about the water of Lake Superior, as well as the wide variety of fish found there. There are also photos and many fascinating facts about Lake Superior.

INDEX

Page numbers in boldface are illustrations.
Entries in boldface are glossary terms.

ABOUT THE AUTHOR

From circus science to vampires, Alicia Klepeis loves to research fun and out-of-the-ordinary topics that make nonfiction exciting for readers. Alicia began her career at the National Geographic Society. She is the author of numerous children's books including *Bizarre Things We've Called Medicine*, *Goblins*, *Understanding Saudi Arabia Today*, and *The World's Strangest Foods*. Alicia is currently working on several projects involving unusual animals, American history, and paranormal experiences. She has visited a number of cool lakes including Lake Tahoe, Lake Pontchartrain, and Bassenthwaite Lake (located in England's Lake District). Alicia lives with her family in upstate New York.

PHOTO CREDITS